SIRENS AND RAIN

SIRENS AND RAIN

Poems by
Barry George

Accents Publishing • Lexington, Kentucky • 2020

Printed in the United States of America

Accents Publishing
Editor: Katerina Stoykova-Klemer
Cover Photograph: Barry George

Library of Congress Control Number: 2020950277
ISBN: 978-1-936628-62-9
First Edition

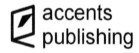

Accents Publishing is an independent press for brilliant voices. For a catalog of current and upcoming titles, please visit us on the Web at

www.accents-publishing.com

CONTENTS

I. Heat Warning

first skyline—
a single window pane
reflects the sun

city dawn—
window washers
rise on their scaffold

lone jackhammer
rings in the morning
…the heat

street vendor
carries pineapples up
from the cellar

up elevator—
her exit prompts
realignment

heat warning—
the cat's shadow rises
over his bowl

expert deposition—
folding and unfolding
his surgeon's hands

untended fish stall—
the lobsters
stir in their tanks

counting his pennies
in the lunch line—
the comptroller

in between fillings
the dentist again
talks of his son

the coxswain's bullhorn
floats downriver…
summer day

long afternoon—
again at the blinds
the wasp's shadow

extended drought—
the wake of a goose
drifts toward shore

slow conversation—
a passing bus fills
the diner window

the fan blows in
the street's scent—
sudden rain

after the storm
he is rich in umbrellas—
the homeless man

rower's statue—
raindrops hang
from his oars

spurring a horse
amid rush hour traffic—
the Civil War statue

war memorial—
homeless vets
air their fatigues

long deposition—
the lawyer's
at the risk of repeating myself

the cat
reworks his litter—
summer dusk

II. Cicada Season

September dawn—
the almost silent lap
of river oars

sidewalk pigeons
scattering
the day moon

cicada season—
jackhammers begin
the day shift

the white and whiter
shades of a fountain—
cricket song

morning sun—
the limo driver wipes down
one-way glass

school crossing guard
walks home
with her stop sign

Indian summer—
the yellow net ripples
with a goal

river trail—
the shadow boxer whirls
through the maples

North Philly mattress store—
the sign above still says
Joe Frazier's Gym

high over the falls
a heron spreads
the wind

hawk
    letting the wind
    just play

the diva's eyes…
as if
listening

sidewalk stoop—
winos recall
the same forgotten oldie

twilight—
in a second storey window
someone cuts hair

night mist…
police edge out
over the falls

noisy hallway—
the signing class
saying goodnight

wee hours—
the security guard's cologne
roams the halls

sleeping cat—
opens one eye
to listen

a light
in the boathouse—
the long room for the sculls

III. Moon Gazing

night meditation…
the cats roll
my bronze Buddha

el tunnel—
the cloud of light before
a train appears

a darkness
streaked with marigolds—
fall rain

city skyline—
a chill today
in the shadows

pink begonias
deepening
the grey fall

unweeded, overgrown
I sit among them—
autumn marigolds

fall morning—
sequins sparkle
on the girls' hijabs

the darkness
of long-empty stables—
Quaker meetinghouse

overcast sky—
the wobble
in a distant V of geese

city canyons
dark with rain—
a hawk's cry

chalk drawings—
longer rays of autumn
cross the square

in the late sun
of a rose garden
he shadowboxes

the ruddy legs
of the practice squad—
fall rain

November wind
scattering
even the crow flock

police wake—
the cathedral steps
gathering blue

my endlessly climbing
the subway stairs—
afternoon moon

city of phones—
the lost art of talking
to oneself

the vagrant
reasoning with someone
who isn't there

moon gazing—
the sound of our leaky commode
my waterfall

cloudless sky—
the moon at the window
of the space museum

eclipse...
the cats look away
in the windy night

IV. Midwinter Sun

daybreak—
the outline of the city
on Venetian blinds

the drone
of an unseen airplane—
winter sky

first flurries—
both cats strike
hunting poses

the frozen river—
gulls huddle against
new snow

someone shouting
a long way off
in the snow storm

wintry day—
the bootblack reads the paper
with a magnifying glass

cold playground—
even the point guard
casts a long shadow

freezing drizzle—
the colorful serape
of a homeless man

not quite
the tailors I had hoped for...
moths

musty and somewhat
worn around the edges—
the used book seller

December sky—
folding into and out of itself
the crow flock

I was here before—
beneath the sycamores
of winter

midwinter sun—
too close
a loud crow caws

gull's cry—
my thoughts
far inland too

sidewalk valentine—
a heart chalked around
worn initials

once before you go
receding snow bank
tell me your secrets

a turnstile
going around by itself—
winter rain

faint footfall—
the cat walking slowly
toward daybreak

cold dawn—
the night waitress
buttons her coat

V. Bowing to Dandelions

muddy river—
a statue's image struggles
to the surface

first spring sun—
the river gods lounge
in dry fountains

early thaw—
on my favorite student's arm
a crude tattoo

morning shade—
the parking guard's basso
warms the sidewalk

back streets—
the diva's warm-up rises
above sirens and rain

windy March—
his trouser legs ripple
with the jackhammer

off to school—
a father and two
small umbrellas

sudden rain…
a quickening clatter
of heels

the campus in bloom—
my crush on the new
general counsel

dogwoods in blossom—
workmen polish
the somber face of Grant

park statue—
a French general bowing
to dandelions

Easter morning—
even the beggar's hair
is combed and parted

low mass—
beneath the rector's robe
New Balance sneakers

pope's visit—
news anchors interpret
the Mystery

priest
raises the wafer...
my third eye

South Philly in spring—
the hoagie shop's signed picture
of Stallone

diner night—
the ceiling fan twirling
in our teaspoons

railroad boxcars
scrape along the tracks—
a night of cherry blossoms

city lights—
I'm overtaken by my
second and third shadows

opened door—
the darkness lengthens
into a kitten

the stylist
rinses away
the sound of her voice

ACKNOWLEDGMENTS

Poems in this collection first appeared in the journals *Buddha's Temple*: "heat warning"; *Chrysanthemum*: "back streets," "fall morning"; *The Daily Yomiuri*: "city of phones"; *Frogpond*: "cicada season," "expert deposition," "gull's cry," "a light," "musty and somewhat," "South Philly," "street vendor"; *Greieri Si Crizanteme*: "cold dawn"; *Haijinx*: "cold playground," "night meditation," "park statue"; *Haiku Canada Review*: "the campus in bloom," "the drone," "low mass," "not quite," "spurring a horse," "the vagrant"; *Haiku Harvest*: "el tunnel"; *Haiku Ireland*: "first flurries," "sidewalk valentine"; *Haiku Spirit*: "chalk drawings," "the frozen river"; *Hedgerow*: "overcast sky"; *Hermitage*: "hawk," "windy March"; *The Heron's Nest*: "the cat," "city dawn," "cloudless sky," "the darkness," "daybreak," "extended drought," "Indian summer," "opened door," "the ruddy legs," "the white and whiter"; *ko*: "the coxswain's bullhorn," "a darkness," "December sky," "Easter morning," "eclipse," "faint footfall," "first skyline," "railroad boxcars," "someone shouting," "sudden rain," "unweeded, overgrown"; *Literary Accents*: "sleeping cat"; *Mainichi Daily News*: "diner night," "up elevator"; *Modern Haiku*: "autumn sun," "city dawn," "counting his pennies," "morning shade," "noisy hallway," "untended fish stall," "war memorial," "wee hours," "wintry day"; *Neverending Story*: "freezing drizzle," "off to school"; *Paper Wasp*: "long afternoon"; *Point Judith Light*: "after the storm"; *Presence*: "early thaw"; *Simply Haiku*: "long deposition," "pink begonias"; *Snapshots*: "high over the falls," "in between fillings," "November wind," "September dawn," "sidewalk stoop"; *Still*: "the diva's eyes," "in the late sun," "priest"; *Times Haiku*: "city lights"; and *Tiny Words*: "the fan"; in the anthologies *A New Resonance 2: Emerging Voices in English-Language Haiku* (Red Moon Press): "slow conversation"; *Sailing Into the Moon* (Haiku Canada Members' Anthology): "pope's visit"; *The Whole Wide World* (New Zealand Poetry Society): "rower's statue"; and in the short collections *Surfacing* (Haiku Canada): "muddy river," "my endlessly climbing," "river trail"; and *Haiku Canada Sheet*: "moon gazing," "night mist." The following were first published as winners of contests: "once before you go" (Third Prize, Betty Drevniok Contest 2011); "the stylist" (First Prize, Gerald Brady Award 2009); "a turnstile" (Honorable Mention, Harold Henderson Award 2018). "I was here before" and "police wake" first appeared in the chapbook *Wrecking Ball and Other Urban Haiku* (Accents Publishing 2010).

ABOUT THE AUTHOR

Barry George is the author of *Wrecking Ball and Other Urban Haiku* and *The One That Flies Back*. His poems have been published in leading haiku and tanka journals and have been translated into at least twelve languages. His work has appeared in anthologies such as *A New Resonance 2: Emerging Voices in English-Language Haiku, The New Haiku, Haiku 21, Streetlights: Poetry of Urban Life in Modern English Tanka,* and *Bigger Than They Appear: Anthology of Very Short Poems.* Among his honors are an AWP Intro Poets Award, Pushcart Prize nomination, and numerous Japanese short-form prizes, including the Gerald R. Brady Contest, First Prize. A graduate of Duke Law School and Spalding University's MFA in Writing program, he lives and teaches in Philadelphia.

CPSIA information can be obtained
at www.ICGtesting.com
Printed in the USA
BVHW071210270921
617616BV00002B/204

9 781936 628629